Mel Bay Presents Great Mandolin Picking Tunes

Arranged by Joe Carr

Contents

Track	Title	Page
1	Angeline the Baker	2
2	Apple Blossom	3
3	Big Black Dog	4
4	Brilliancy	5
5	Britches Full of Stitches	6
6	Congress Reel	7
7	Cotton Eyed Joe 2	8
8	Cripple Creek	9
9	Daley's Reel	10
10	Georgia Boys	11
11	Little Rabbit	12
12	Cotton Eyed Joe (Old Melody)	13
13	Merry Widow Waltz	14
14	Mississippi Sawyer	15
15	Natchez Under the Hill	16
16	Paddy on the Turnpike	17
17	Pigtown Fling	18
18	The Prettiest Girl in the County	19
19	Redwing	20
20	Rose of Avonmore	22
21	Saint Anne's Reel	23
22	Smith's Reel	24
23	Taters in Sandyland	25
24	Temperance Reel	26
25	Texas Gales	27
26	The Boys of Bluehill	28
27	Tripping Up Stairs	29
28	Uncle Joe	30
29	Wagoner	31
30	Whiskey Before Breakfast	32

1 2 3 4 5 6 7 8 9 0

© 2003 BY MEL BAY PUBLICATIONS, INC., PACIFIC, MO 63069.
ALL RIGHTS RESERVED. INTERNATIONAL COPYRIGHT SECURED. B.M.I. MADE AND PRINTED IN U.S.A.
No part of this publication may be reproduced in whole or in part, or stored in a retrieval system, or transmitted in any form or by any means, electronic, mechanical, photocopy, recording, or otherwise, without written permission of the publisher.

Visit us on the Web at www.melbay.com — E-mail us at email@melbay.com

Angeline the Baker

Fiddle Tune

Apple Blossom

Fiddle Tune

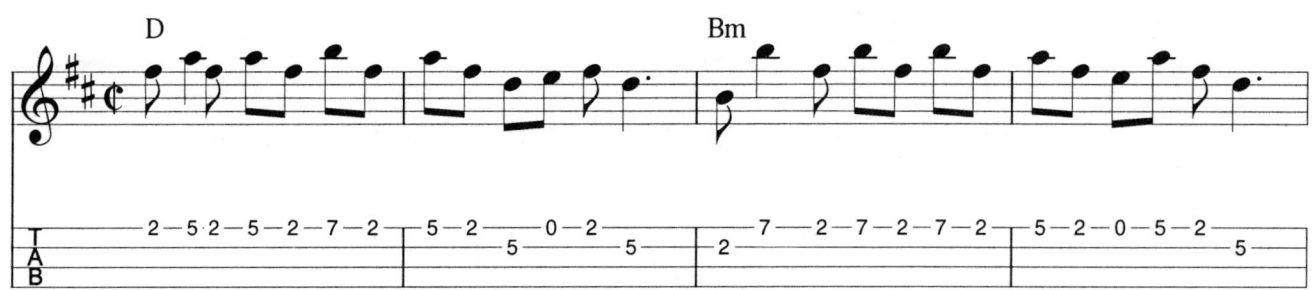
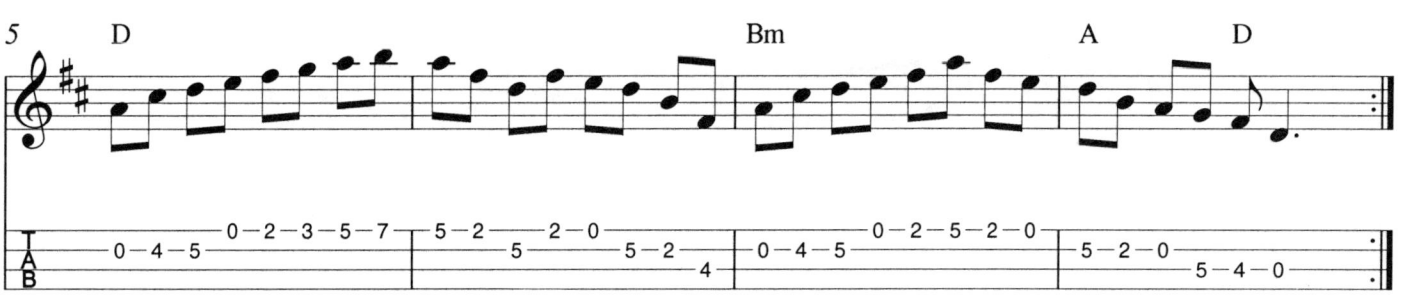

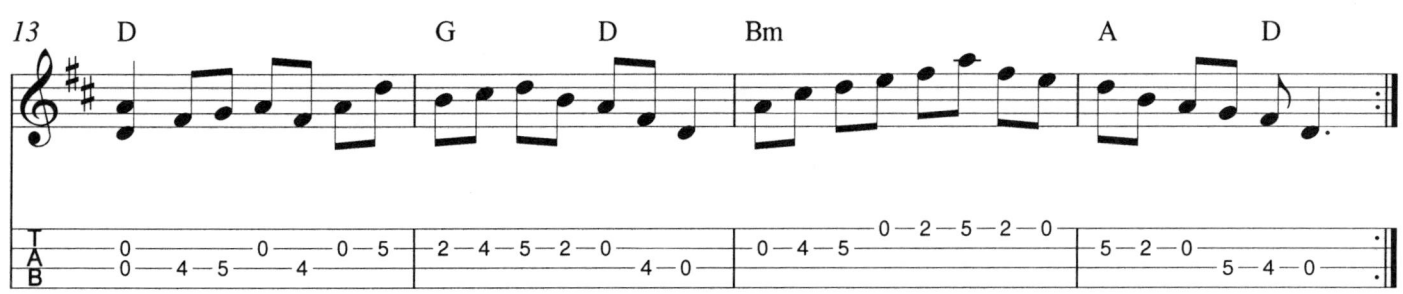

Big Black Dog

Joe Carr

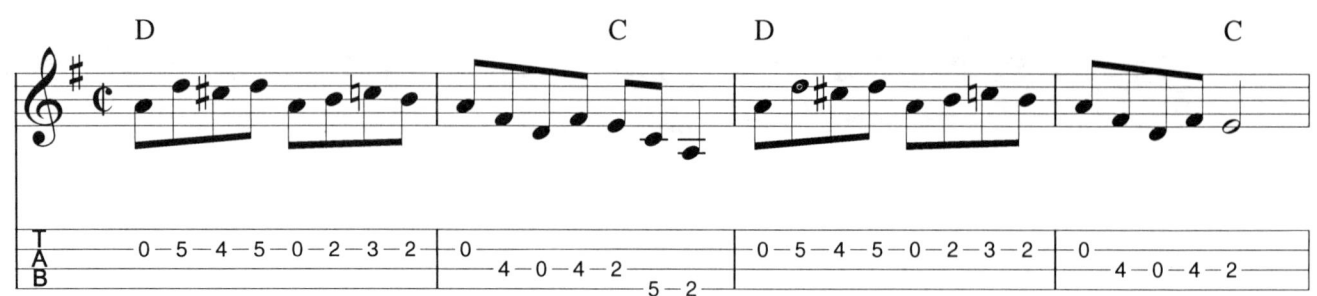
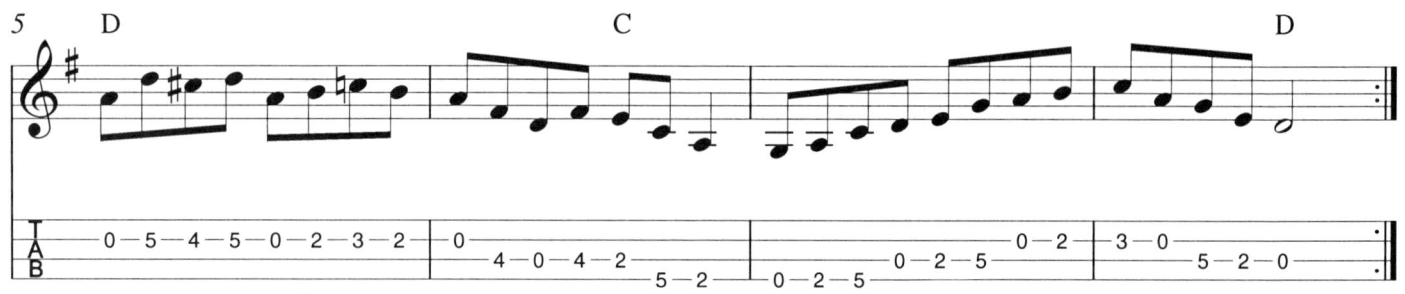

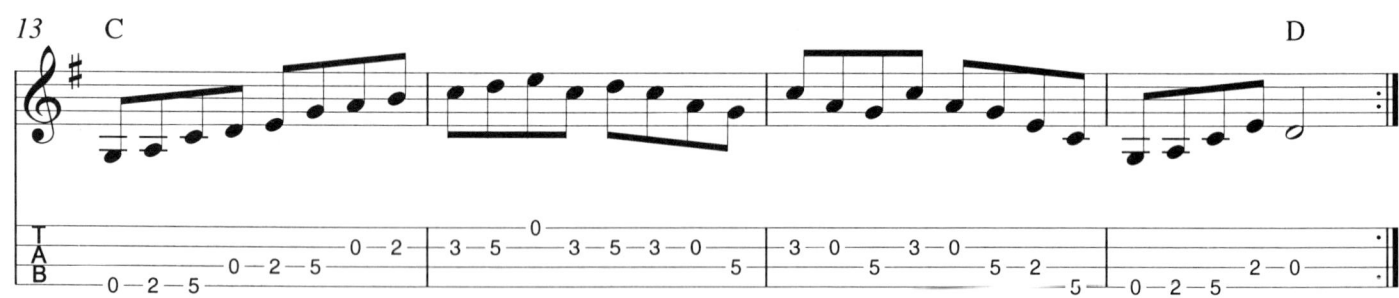

Brilliancy

Fiddle Tune

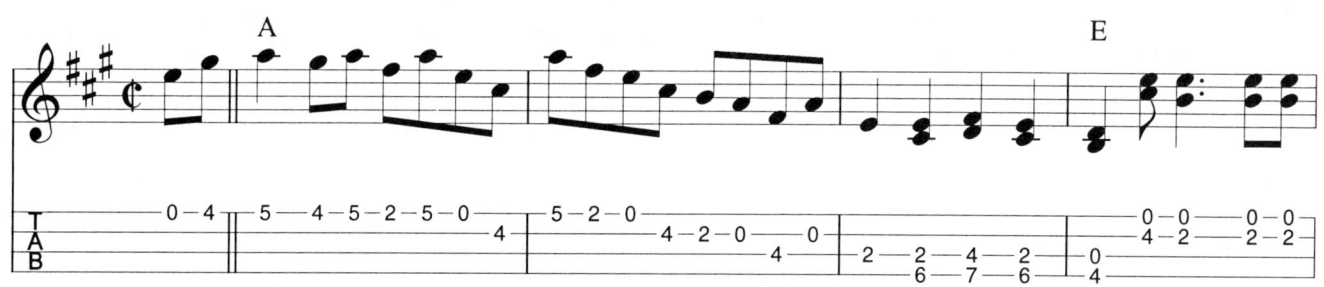
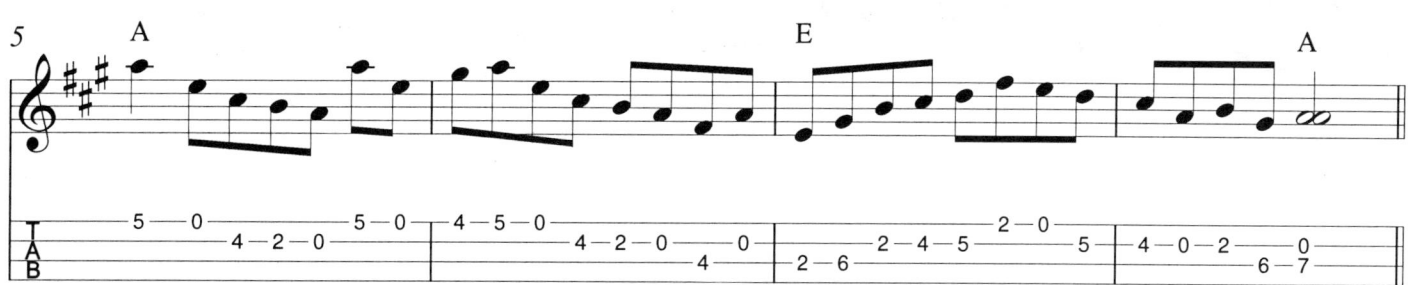

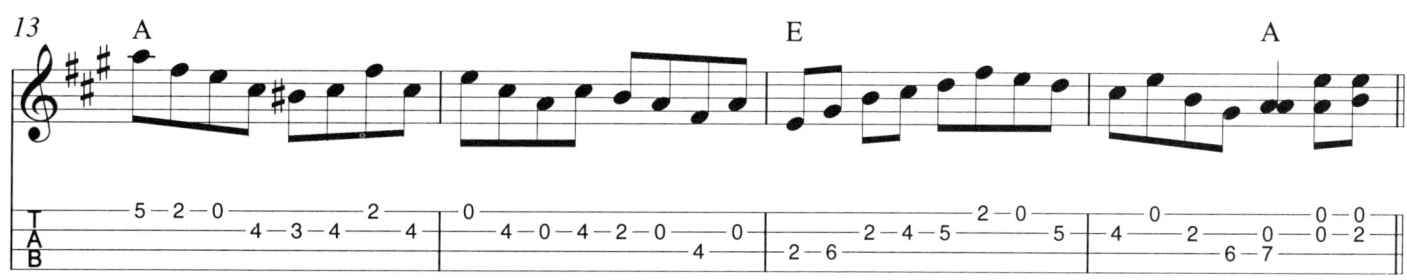
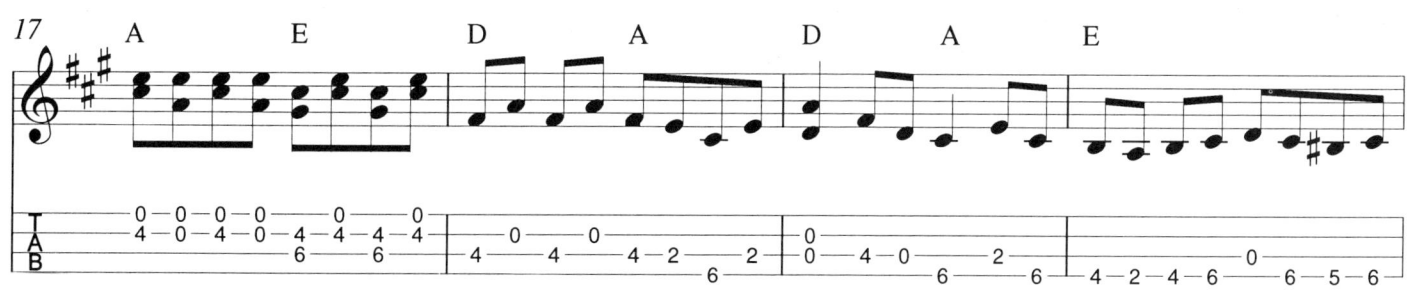
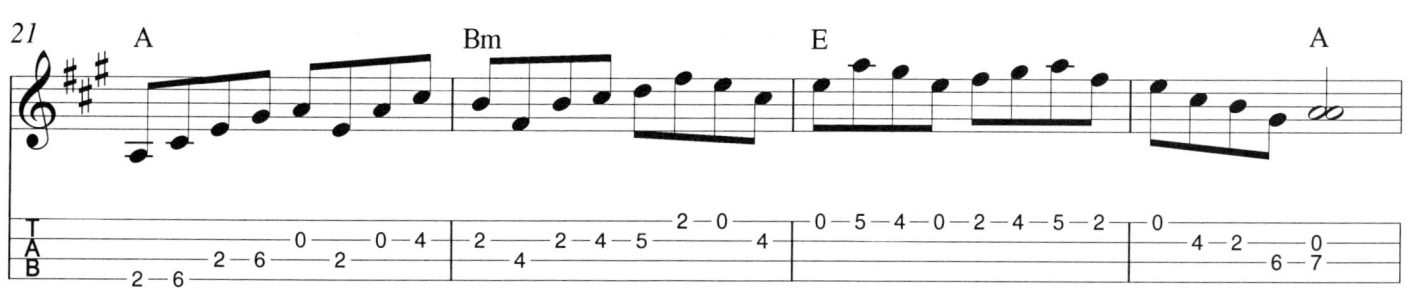

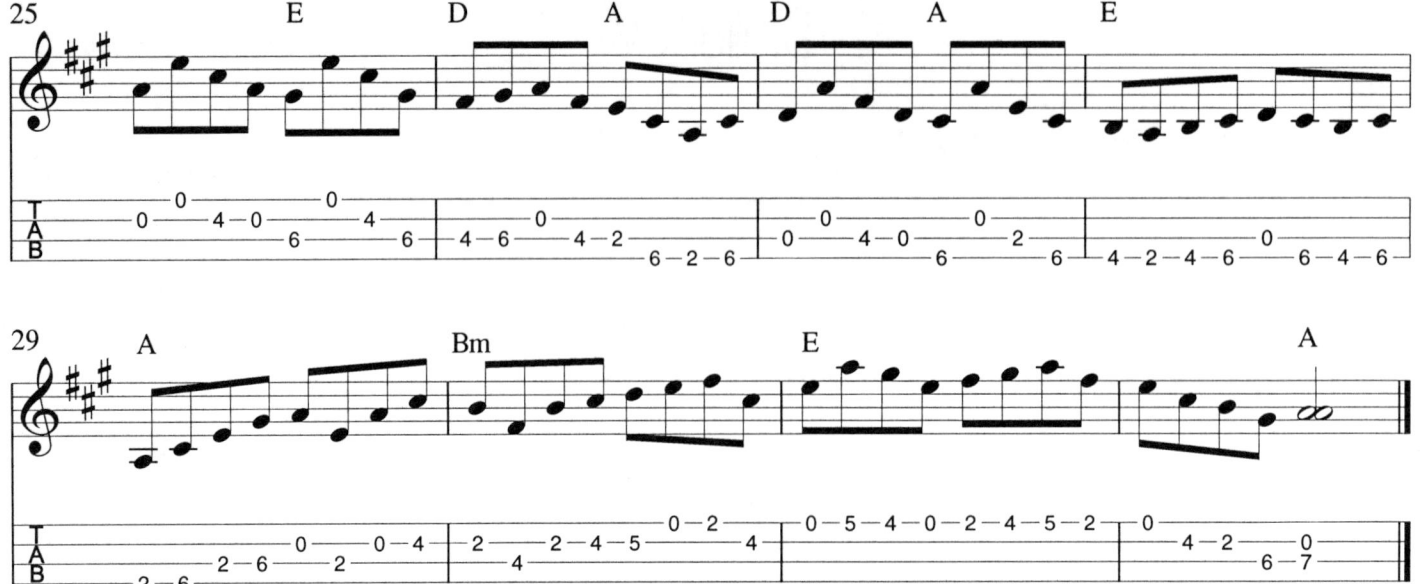

Britches Full of Stitches

Polka

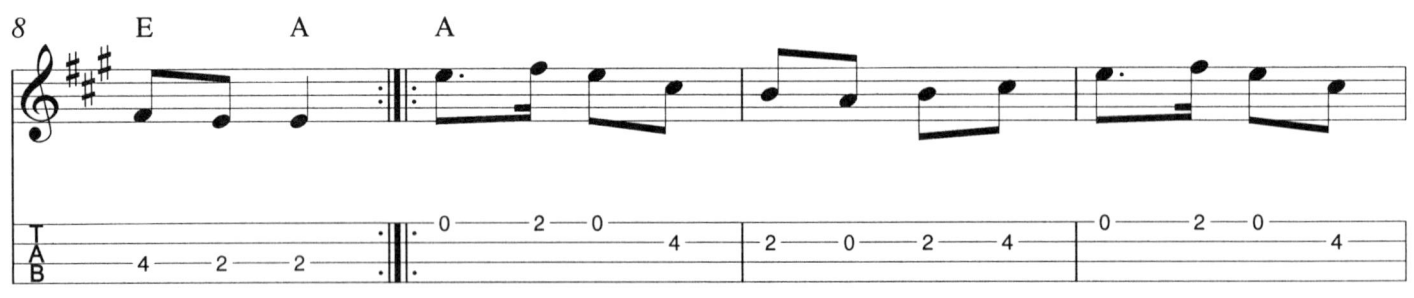

Congress Reel

Irish

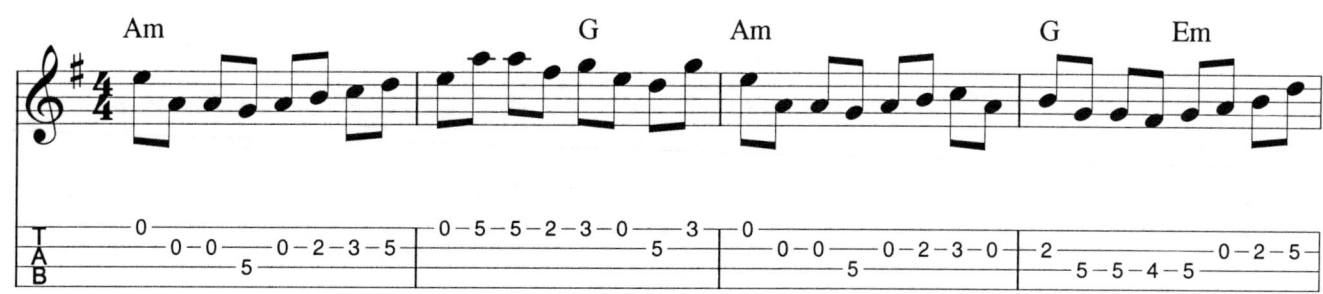
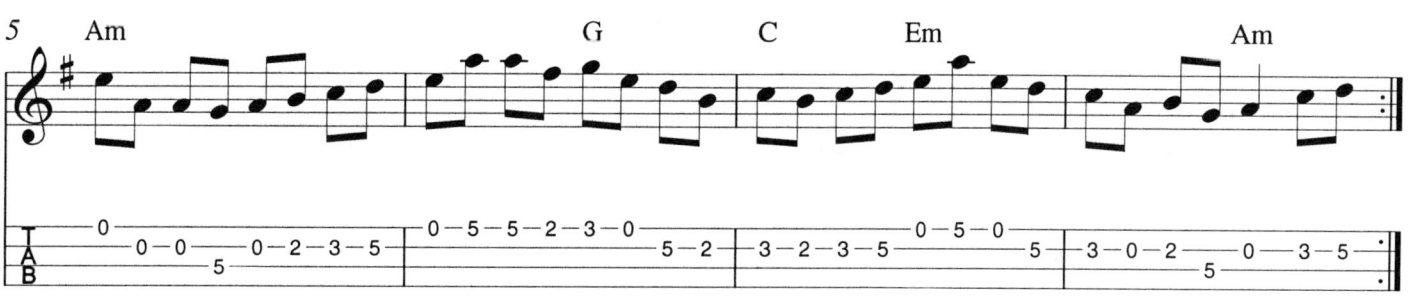
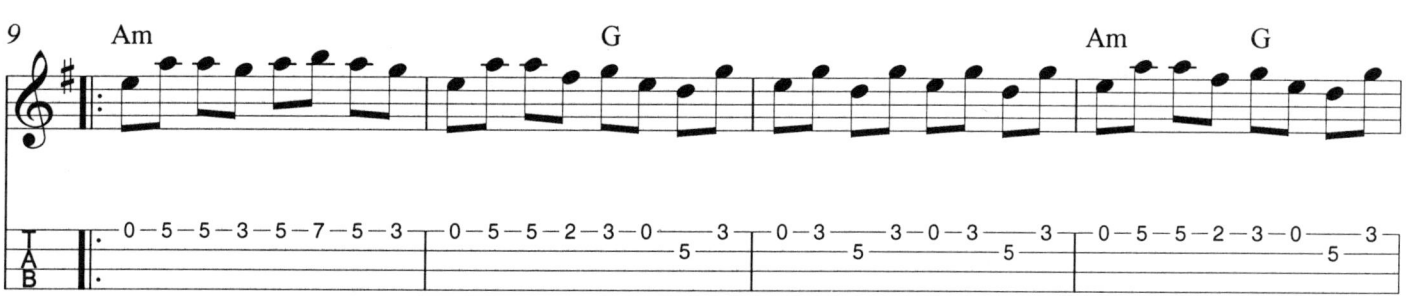
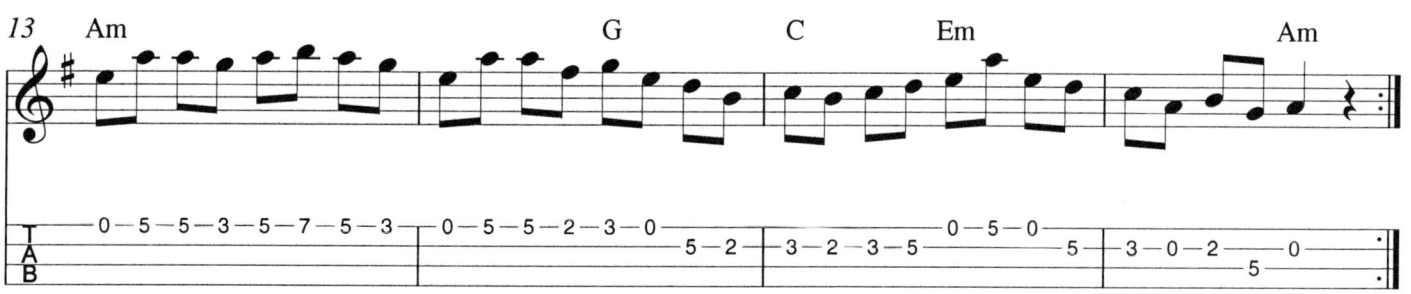

Cotton Eyed Joe 2

Dance Melody

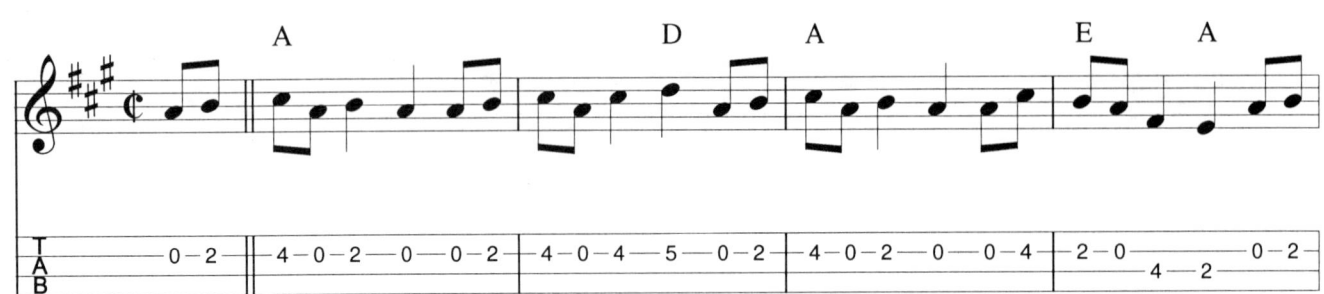
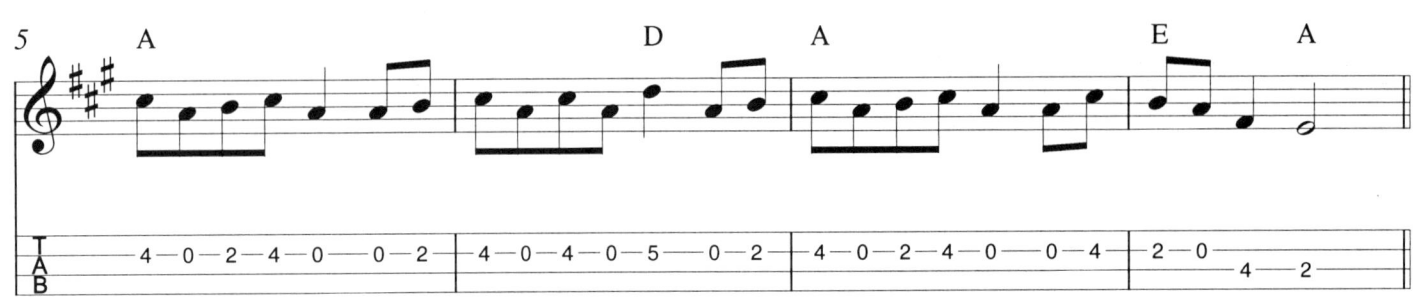

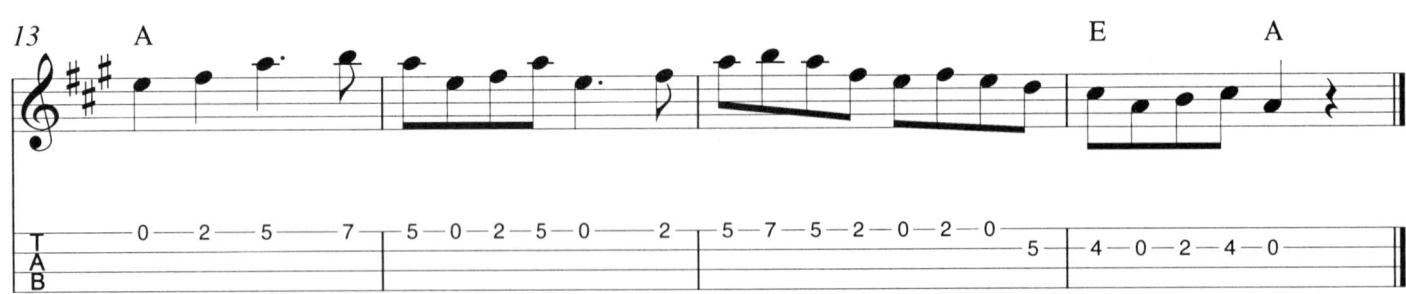

Cripple Creek

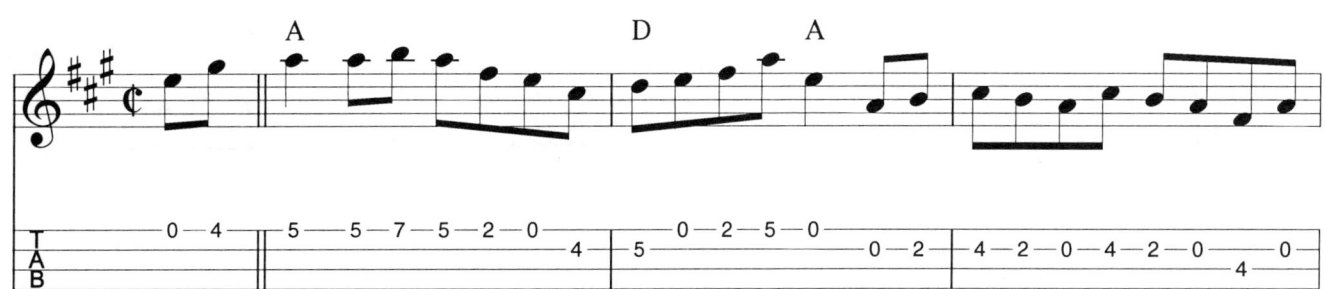
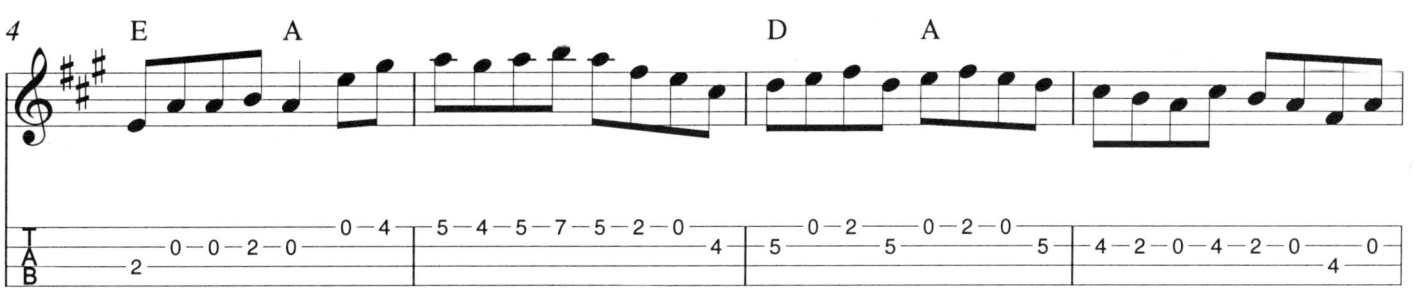

Daley's Reel

Fiddle Tune

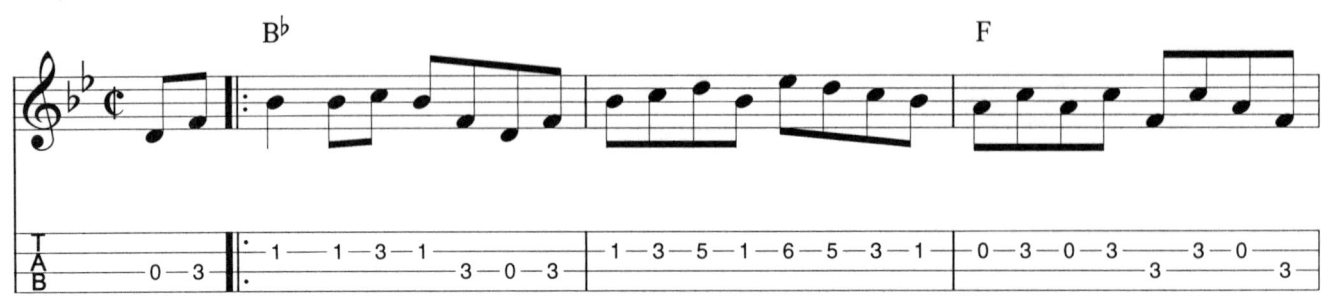
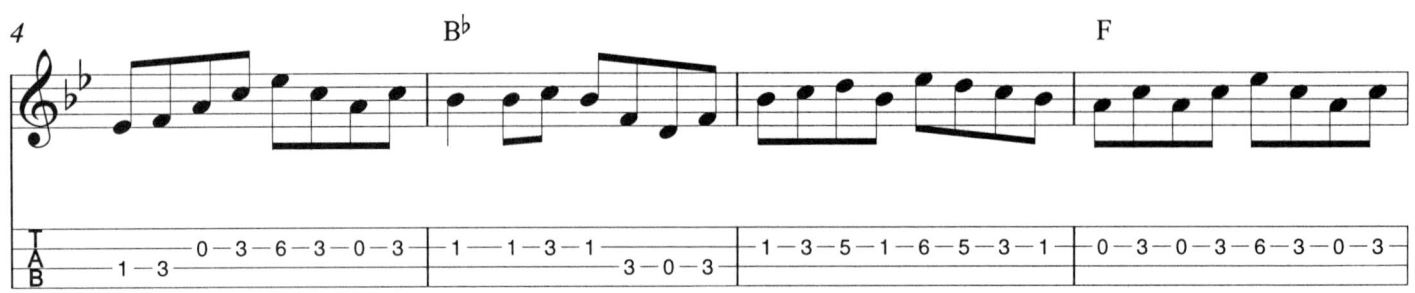
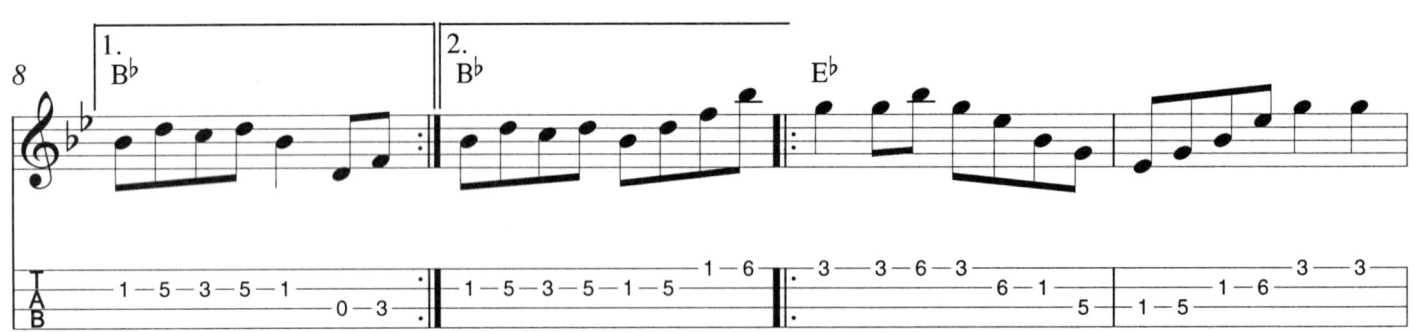

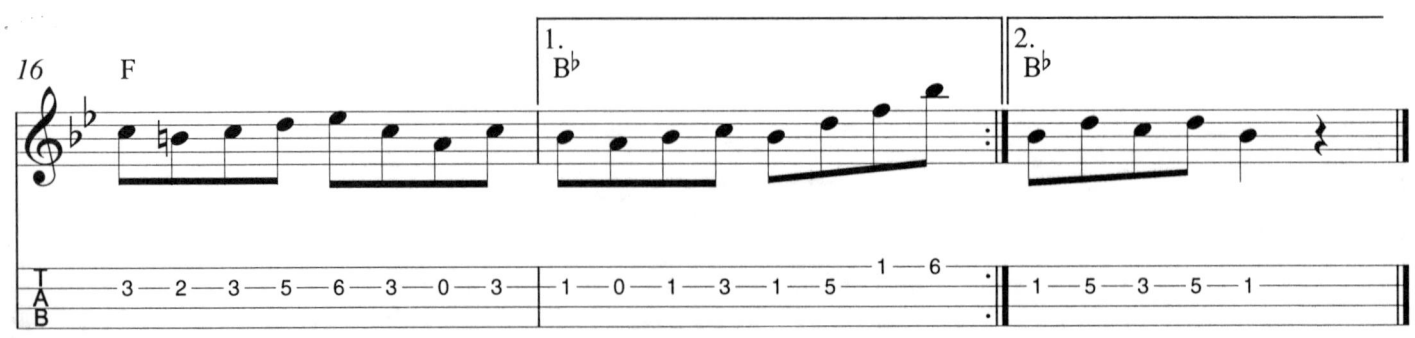

Georgia Boys

Fiddle Tune

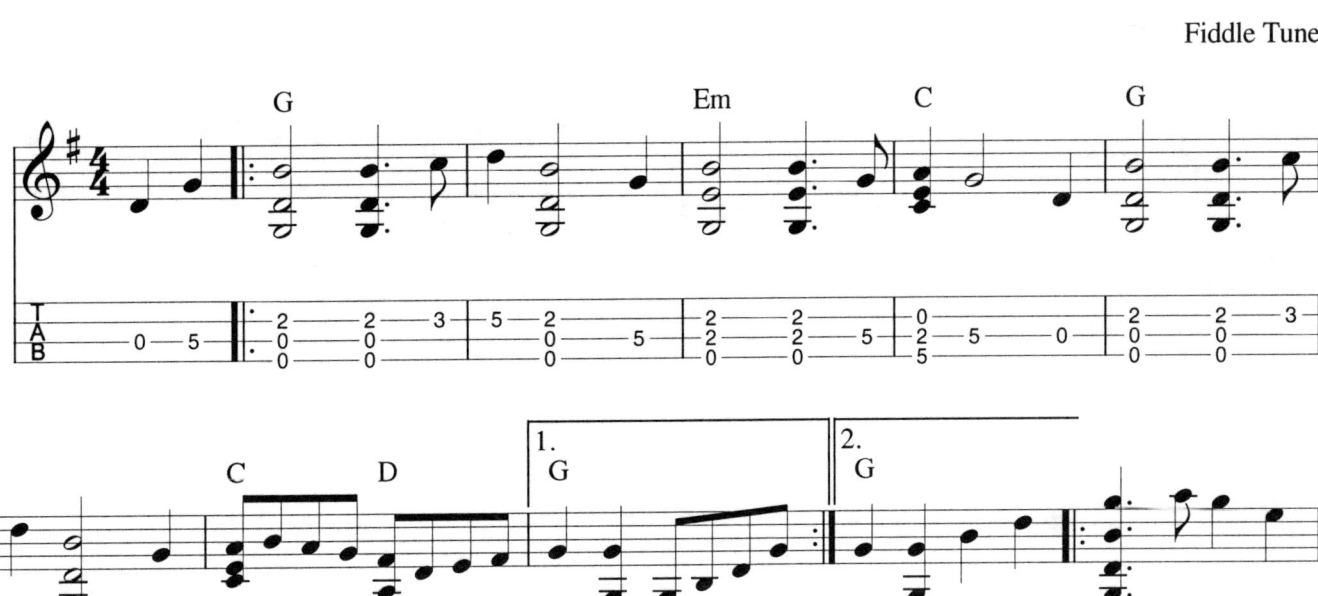

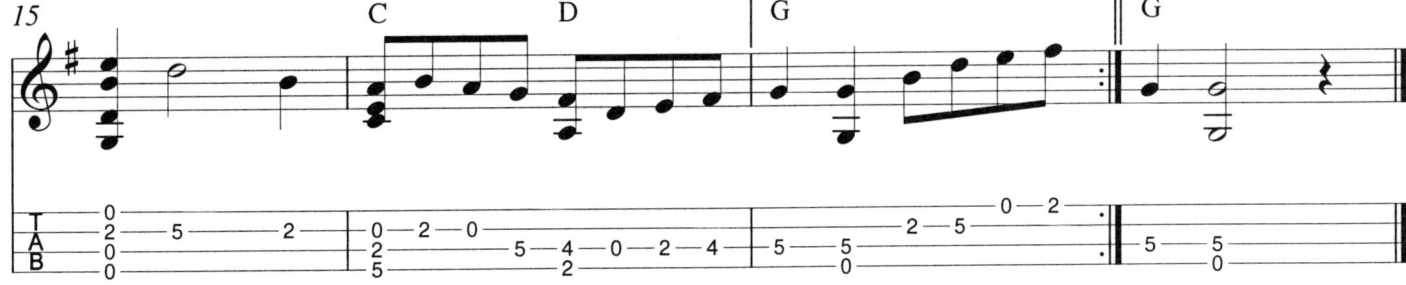

Little Rabbit

Fiddle Tune

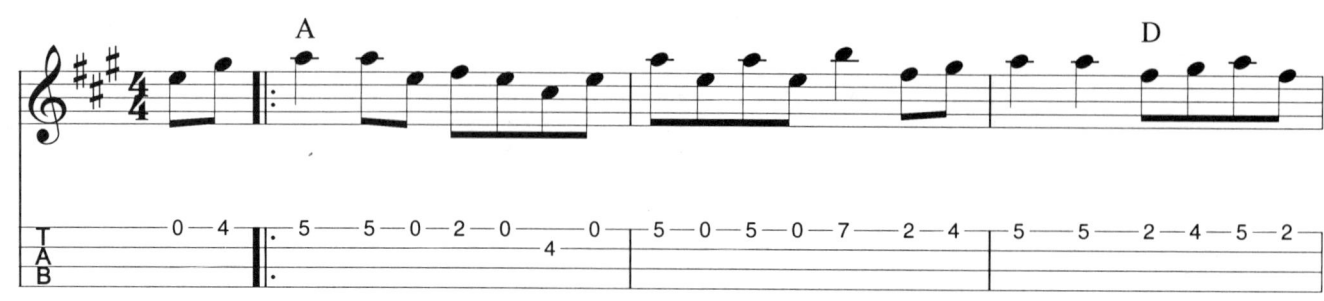
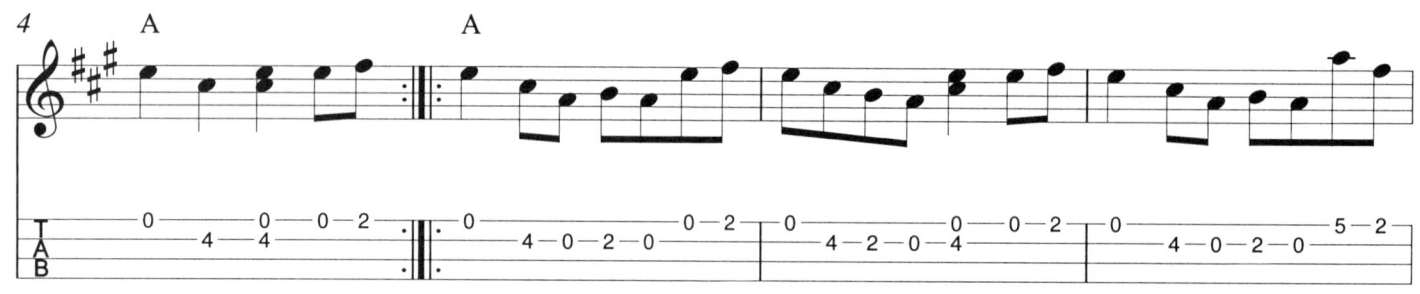
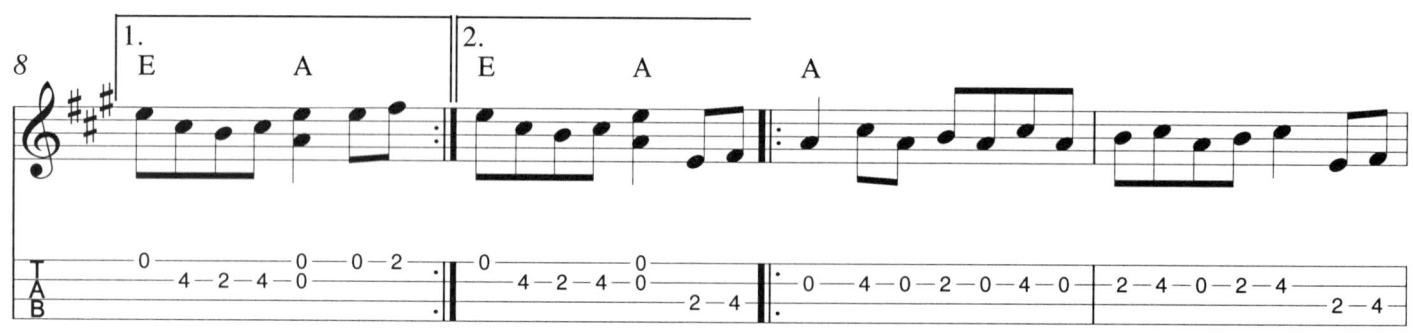
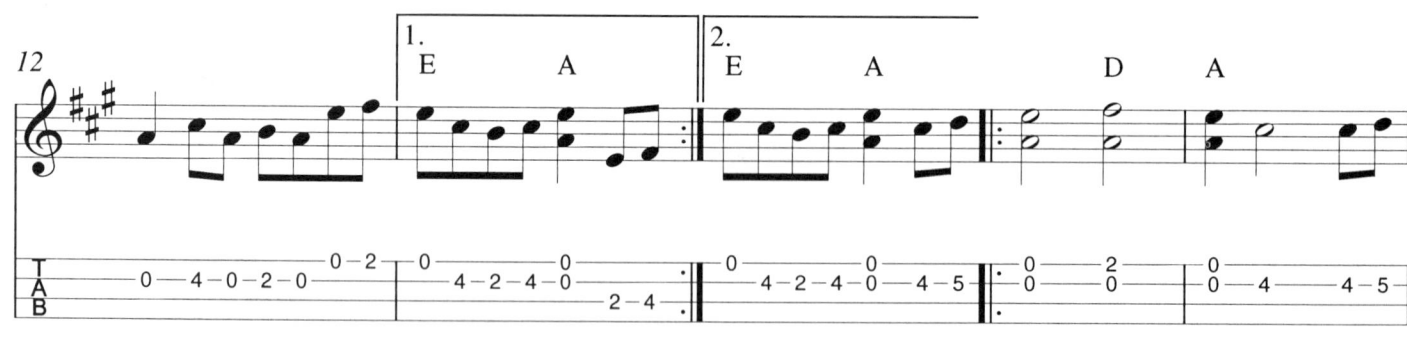
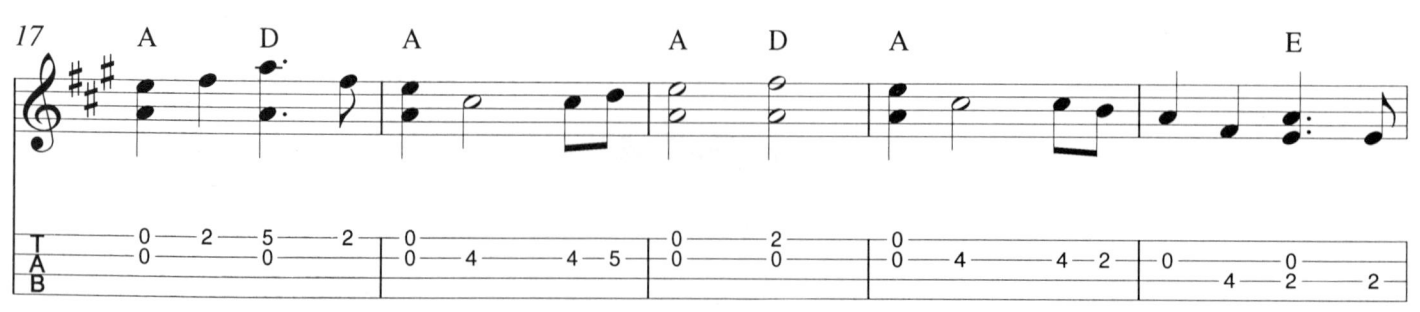

Cotton Eyed Joe

Old Melody

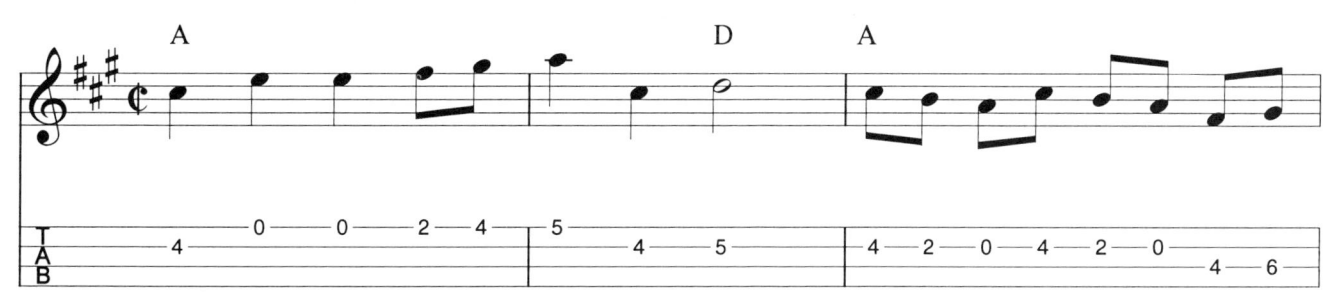

Merry Widow Waltz

Mississippi Sawyer

Fiddle Tune

Natchez Under the Hill

Fiddle Tune

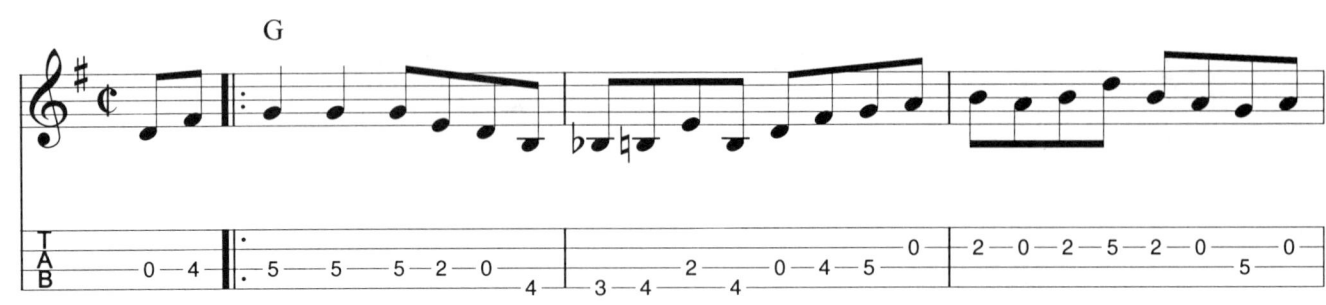
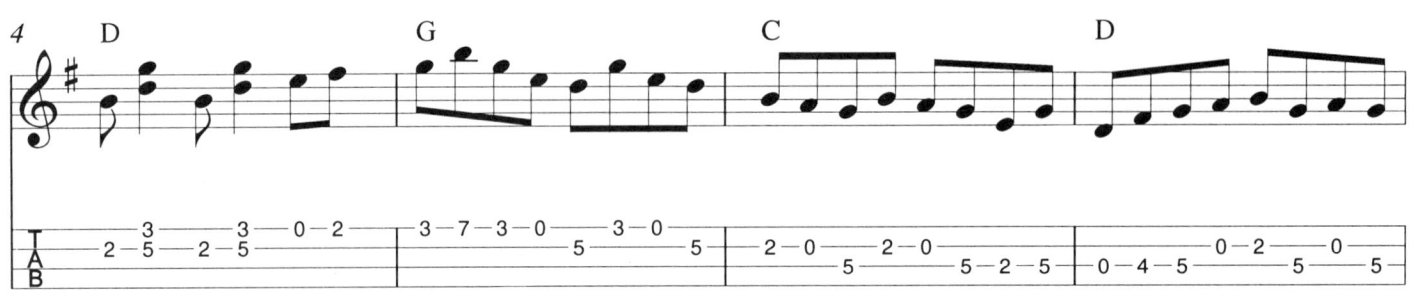
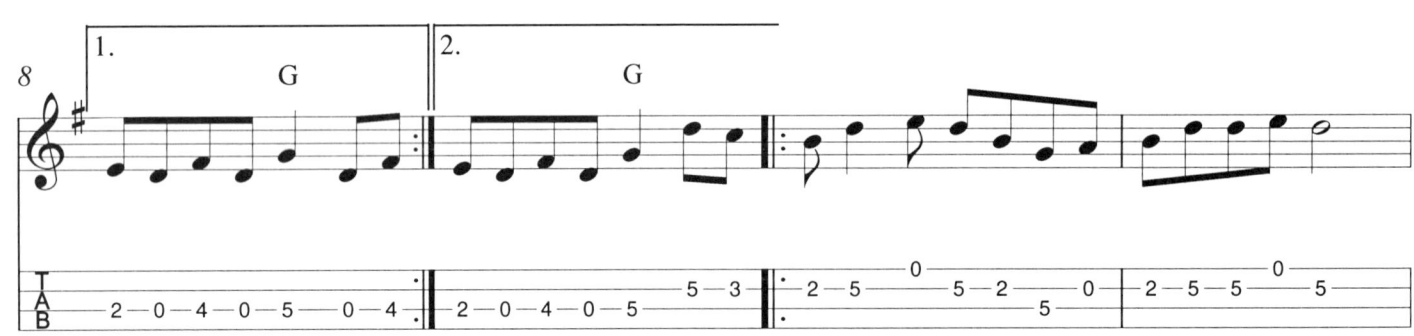
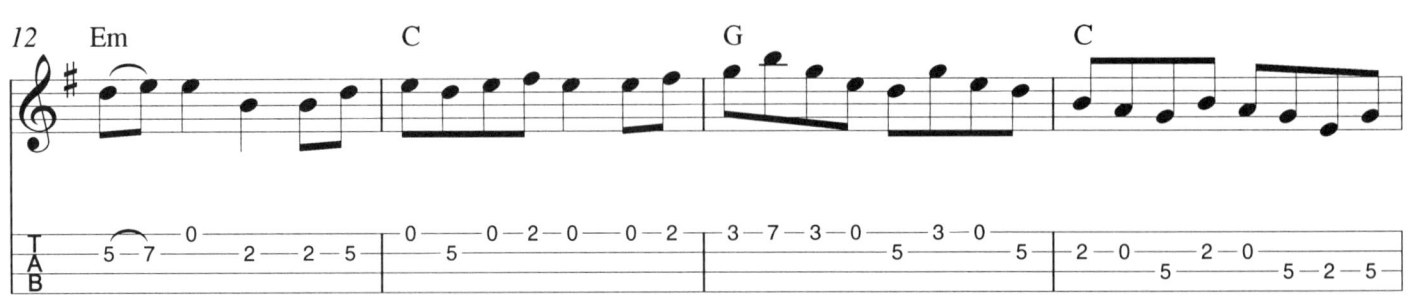

Paddy on the Turnpike

Fiddle Tune

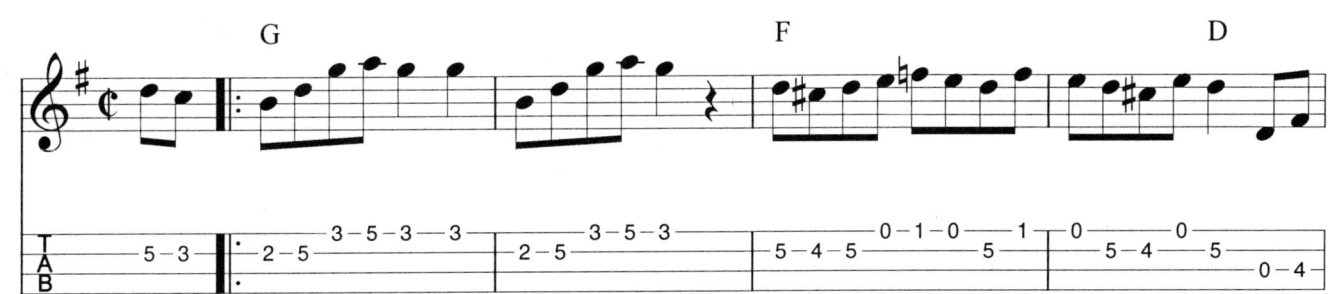
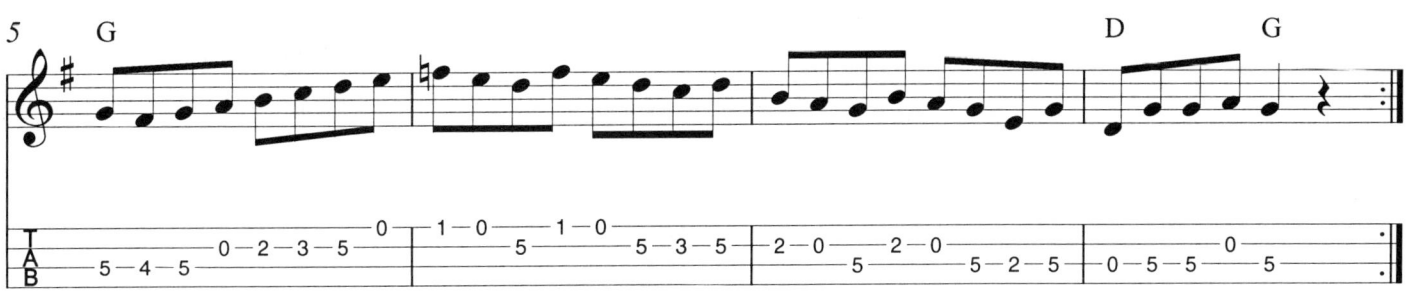

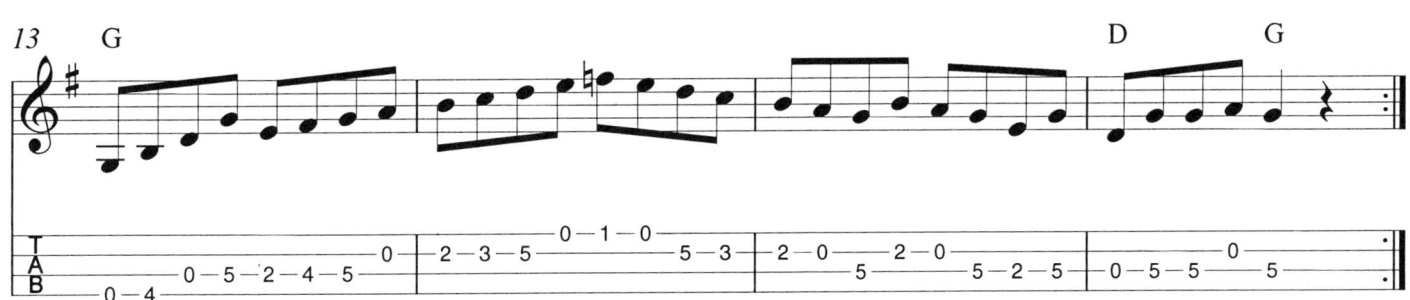

Pigtown Fling

Reel

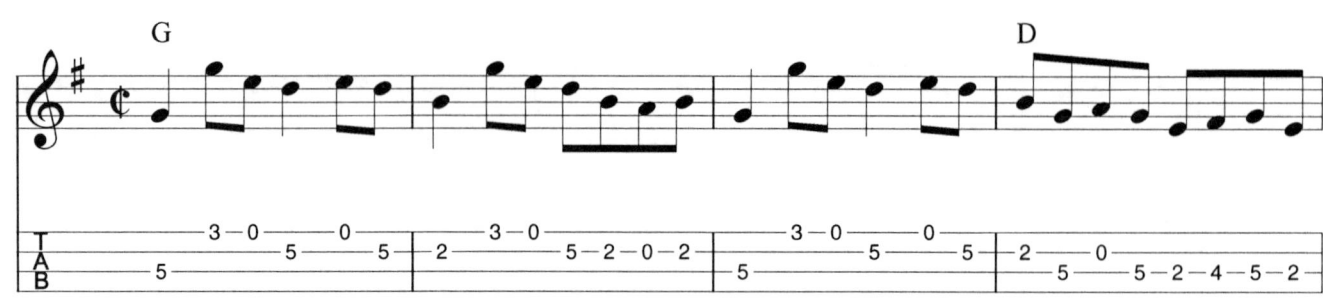

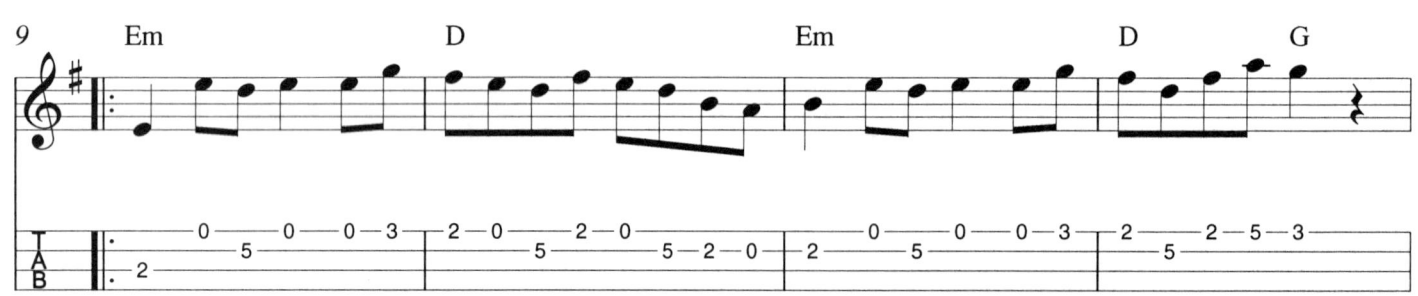
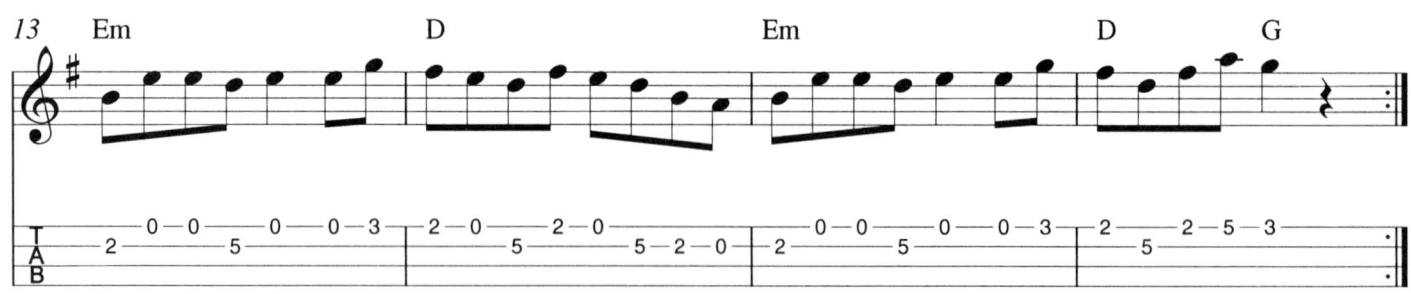

The Prettiest Girl in the County

Fiddle Tune

Redwing

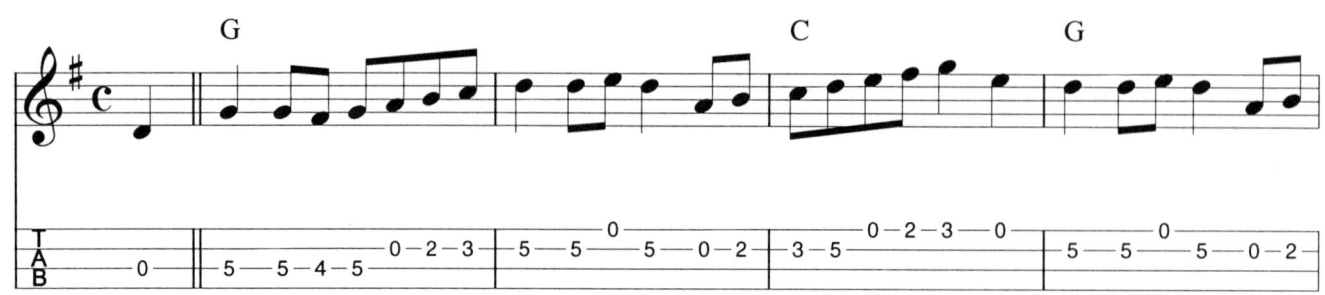

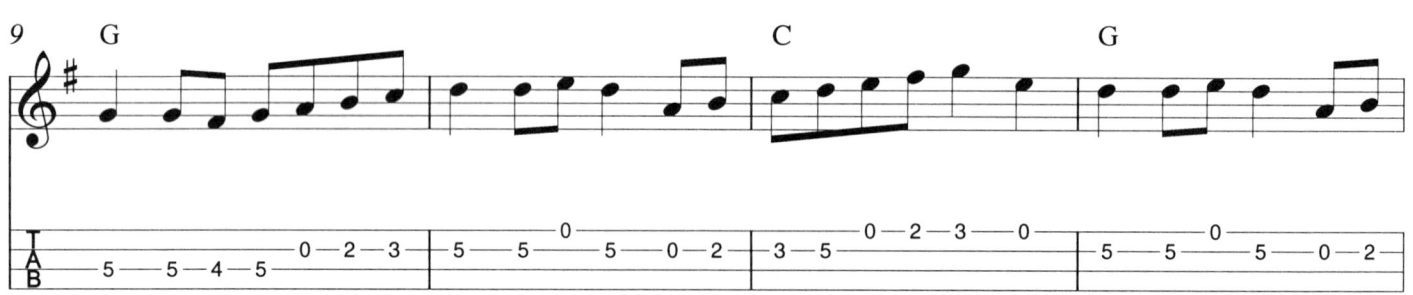
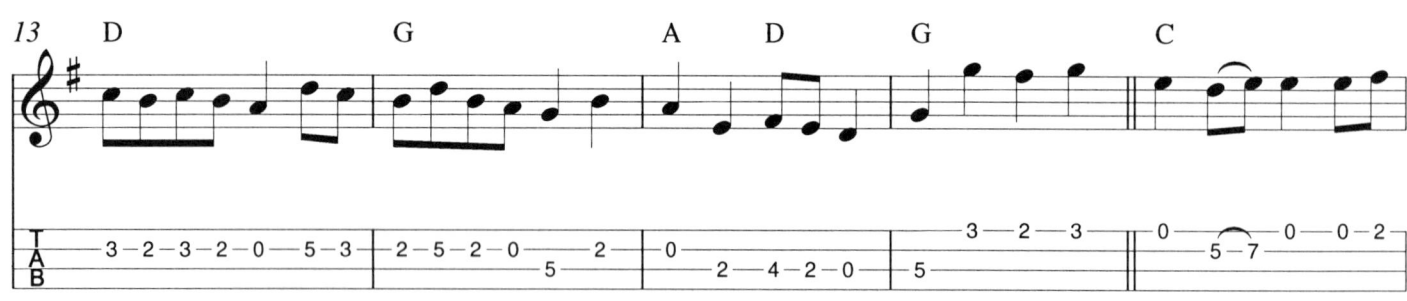

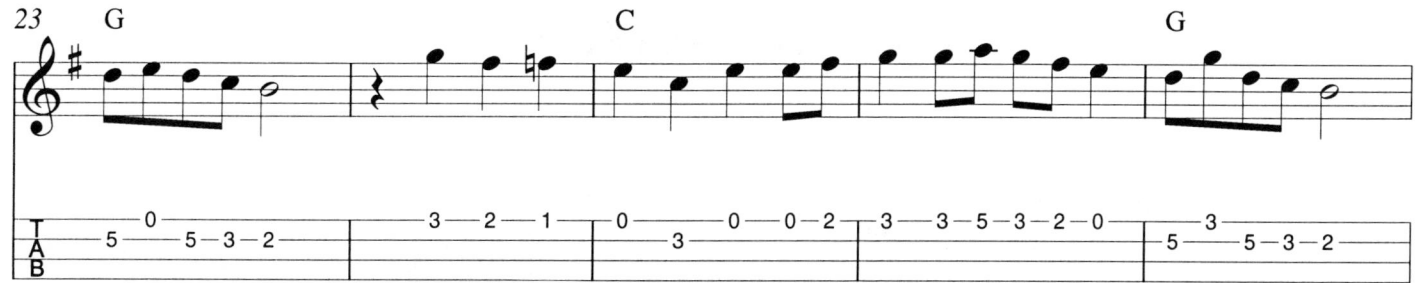
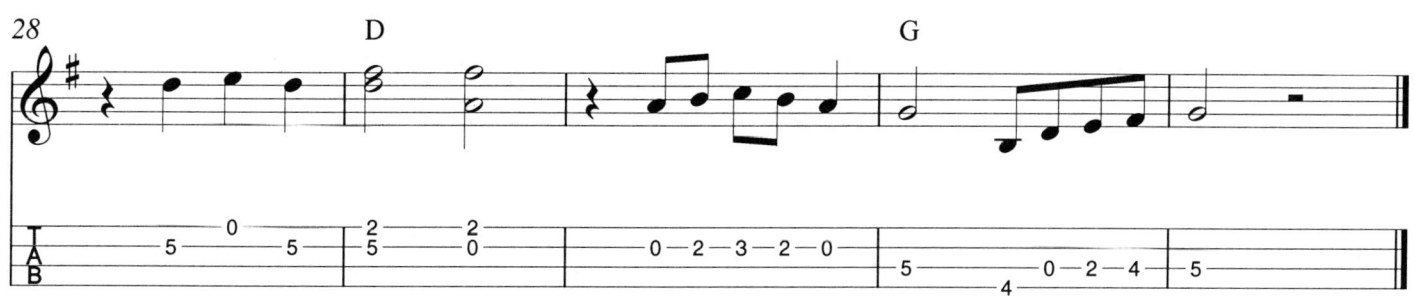

Rose of Avonmore

Saint Anne's Reel

Smith's Reel

Fiddle Tune

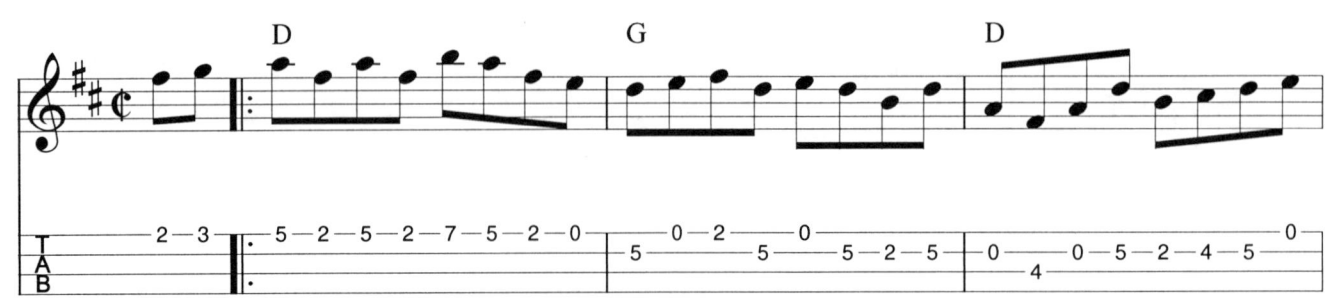
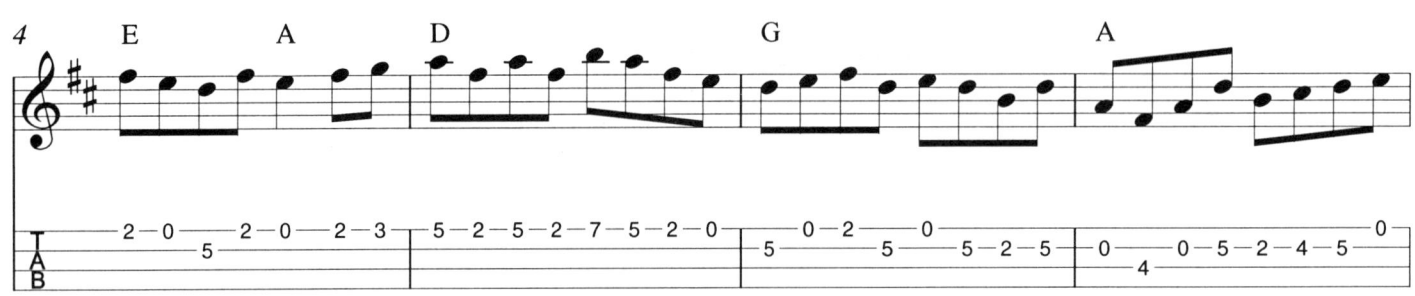
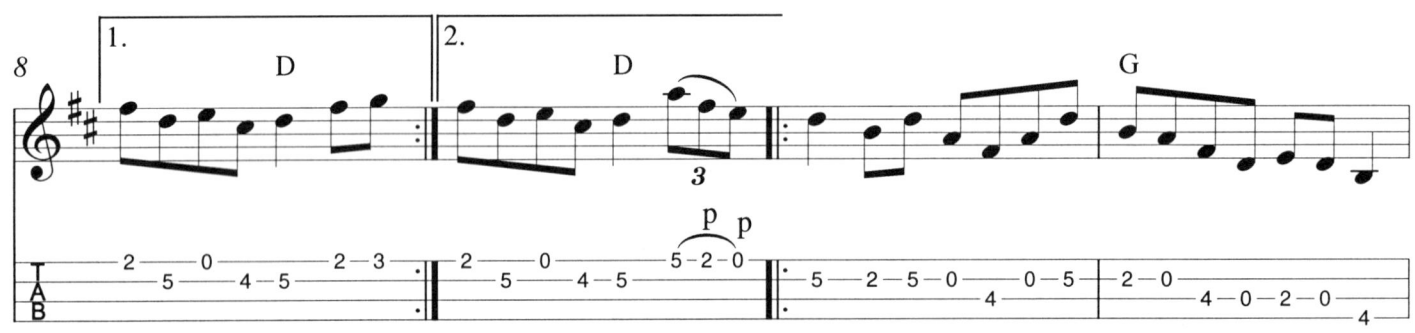
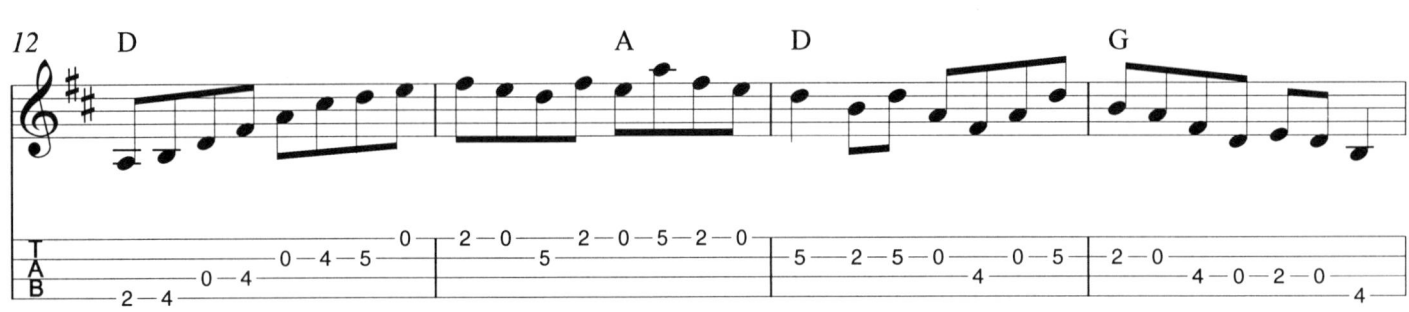
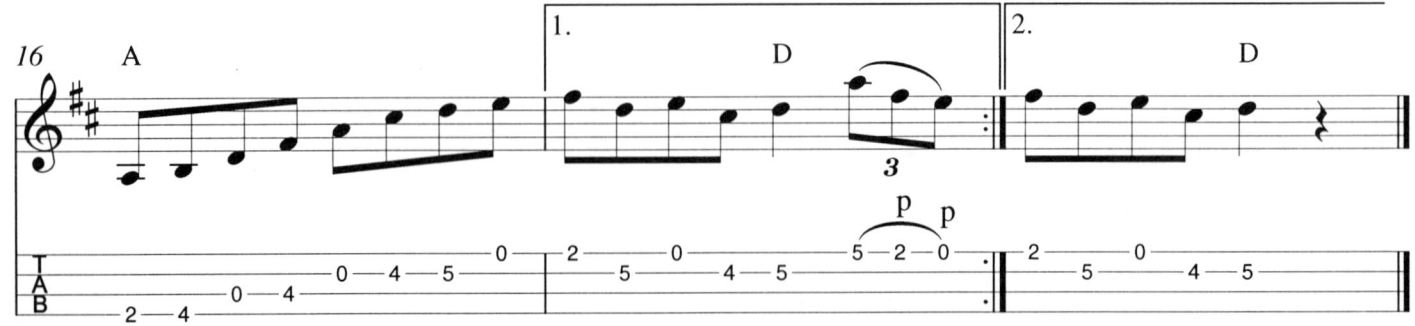

Taters in Sandyland

Fiddle Tune

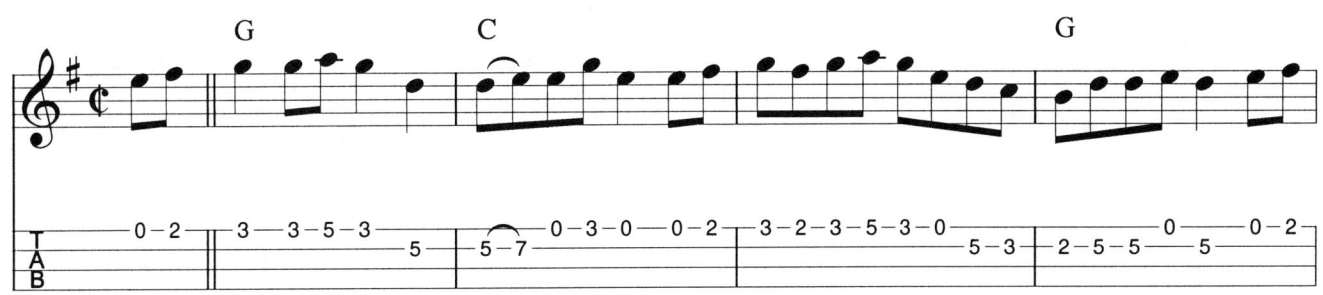

Temperance Reel

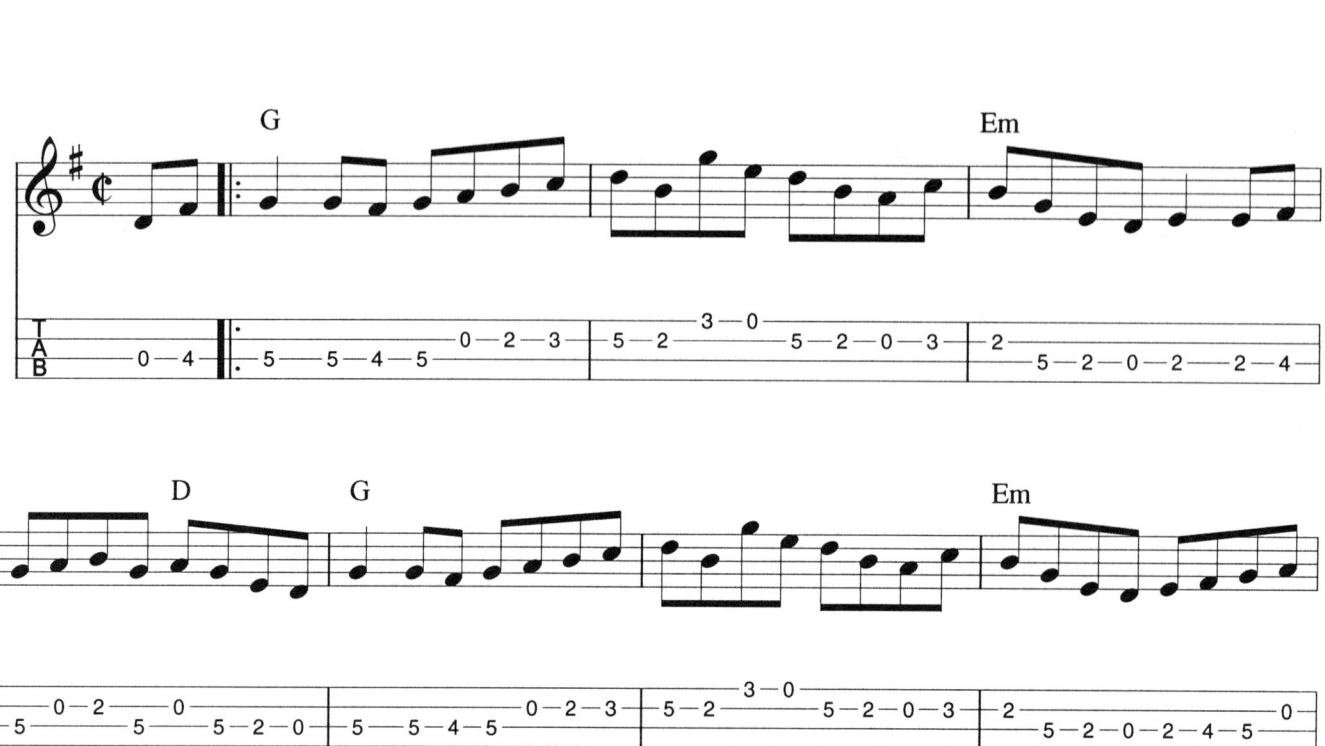
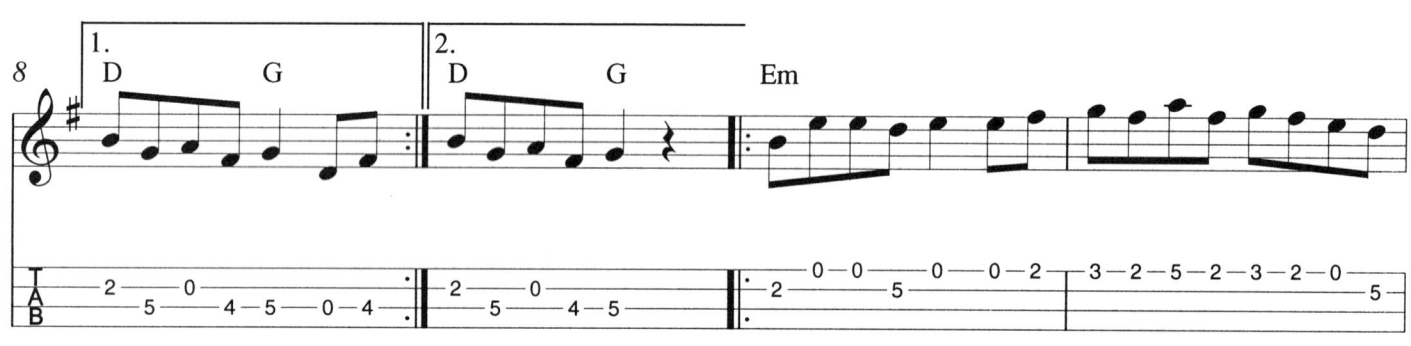
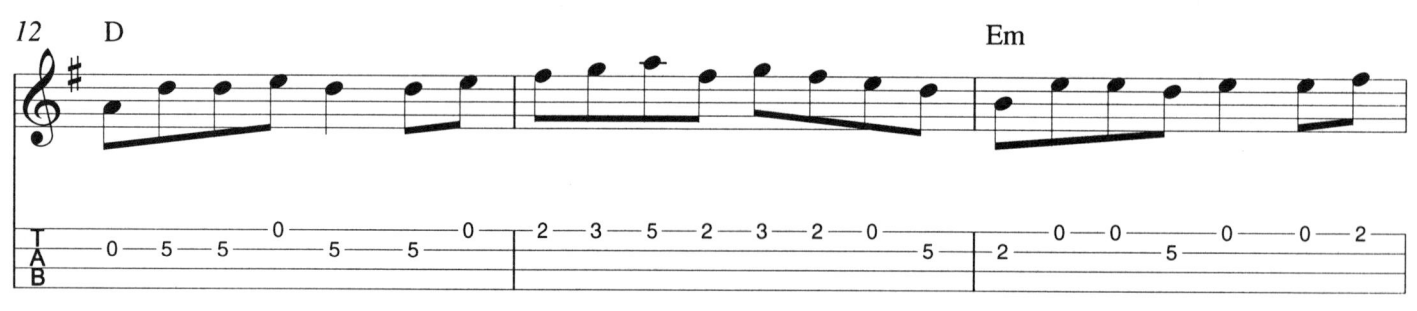

Texas Gales

The Boys of Bluehill

Tripping Up Stairs

Irish Jig

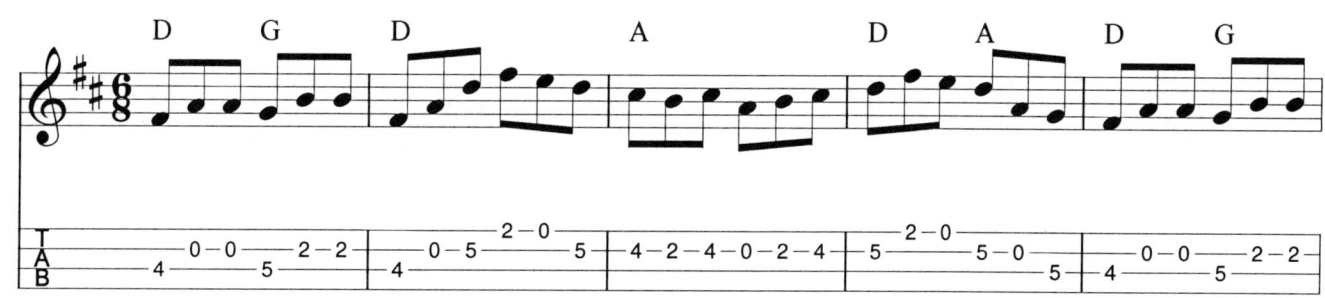

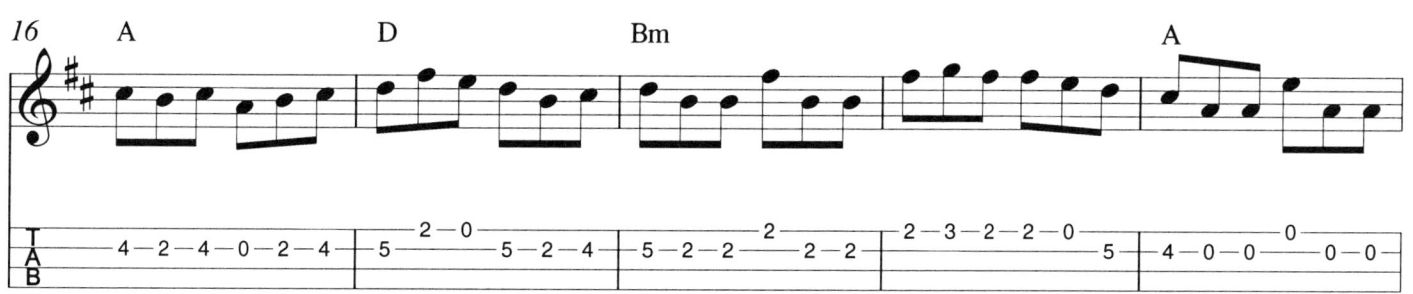
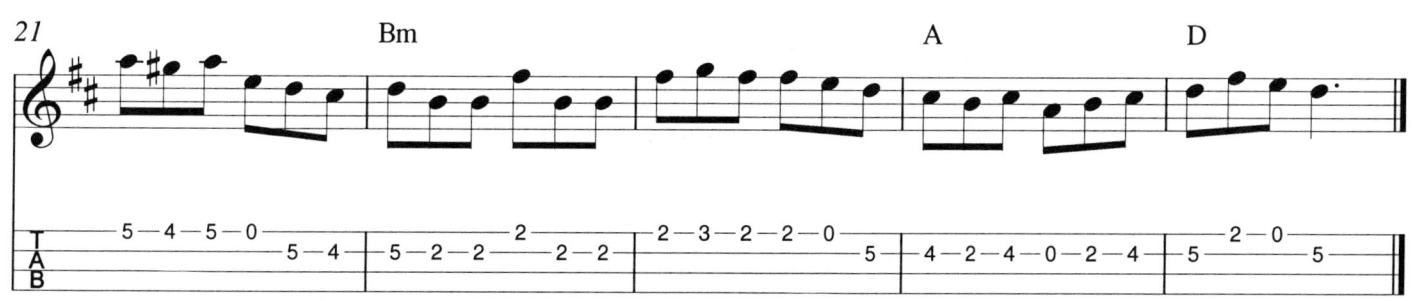

Uncle Joe

Fiddle Tune

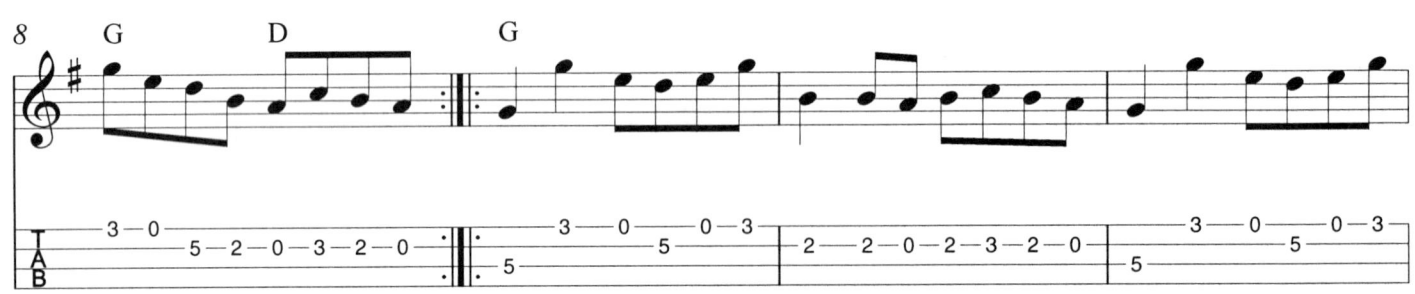
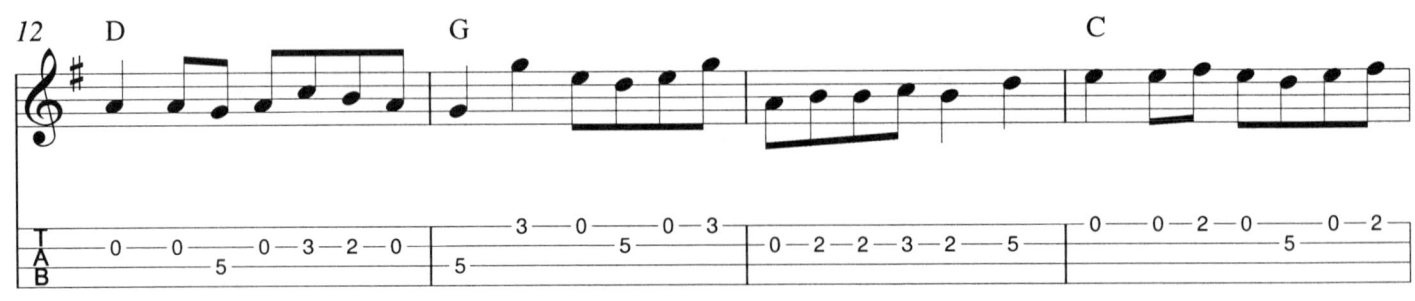
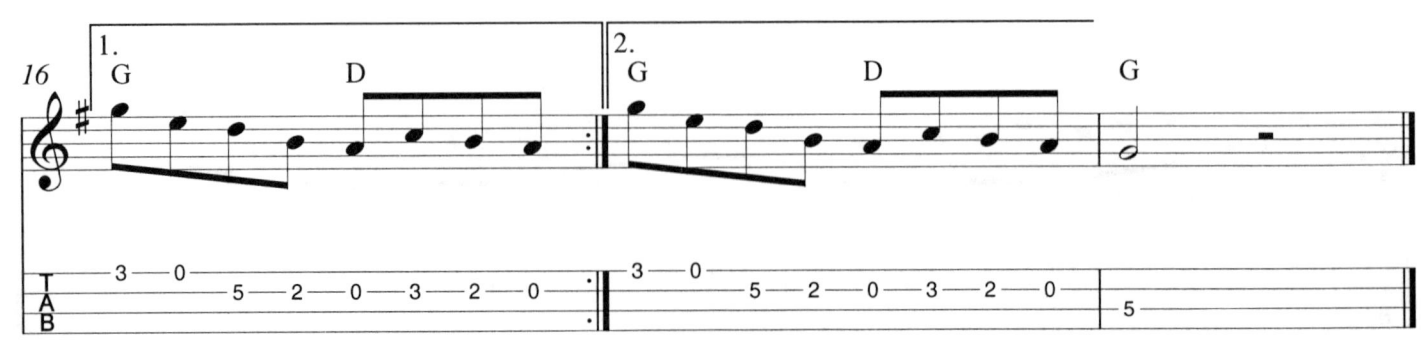

Wagoner

Fiddle Tune

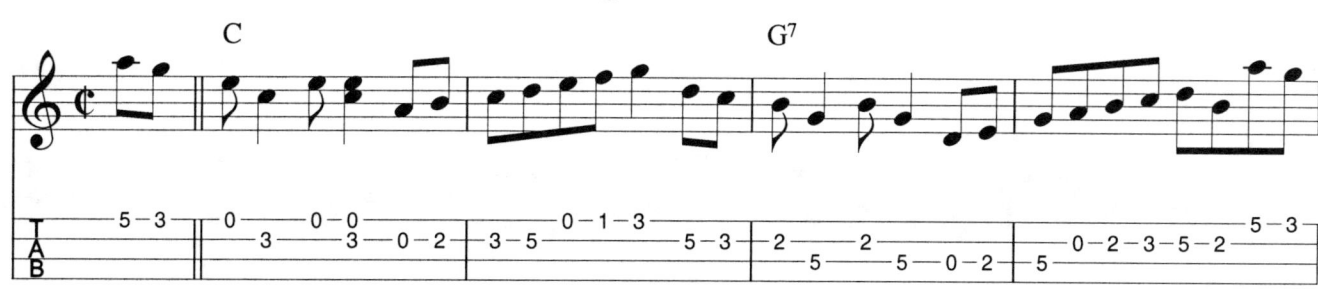
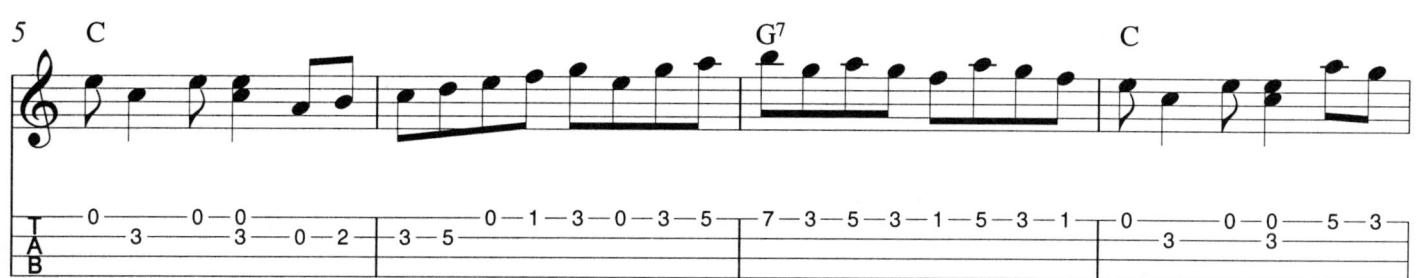
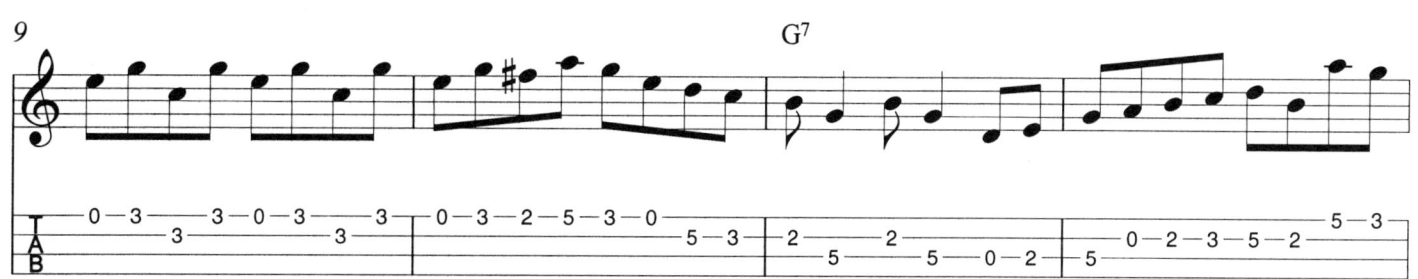
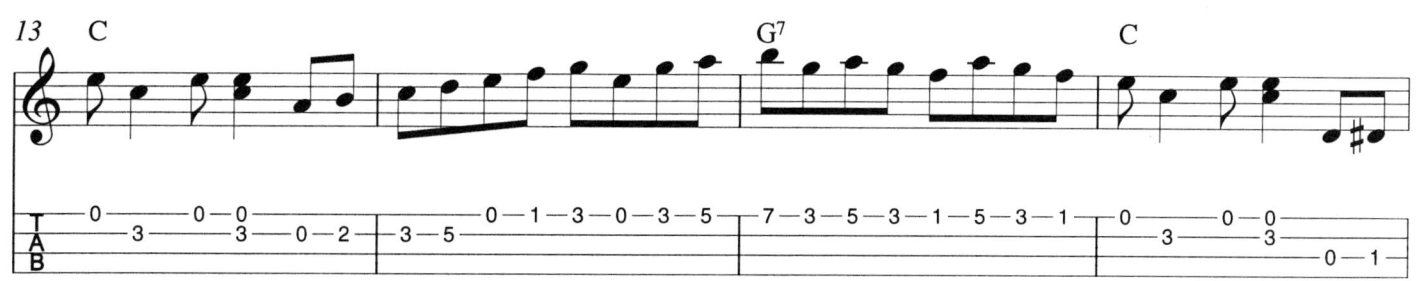
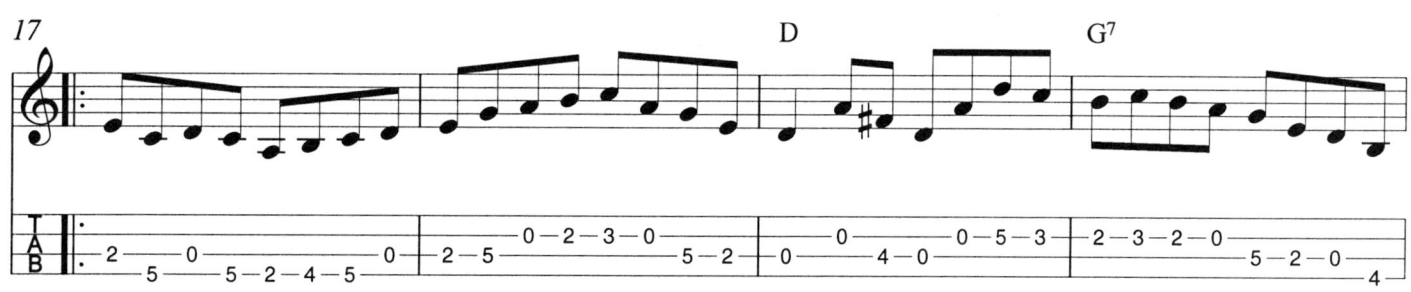
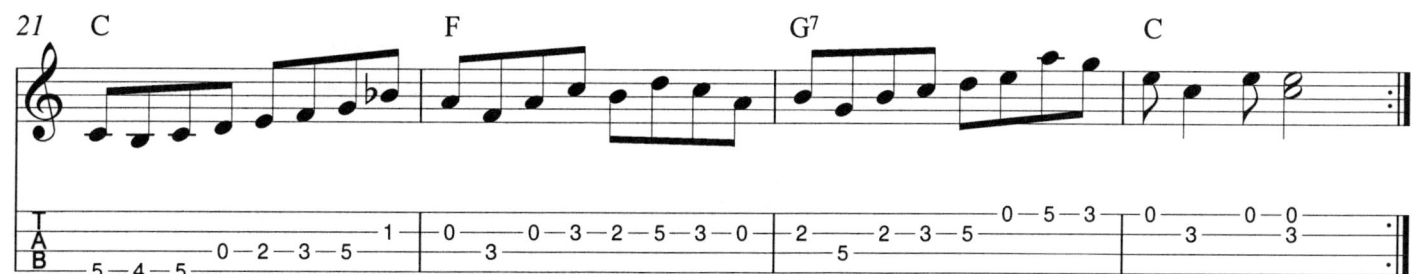

Whiskey Before Breakfast

Fiddle Tune

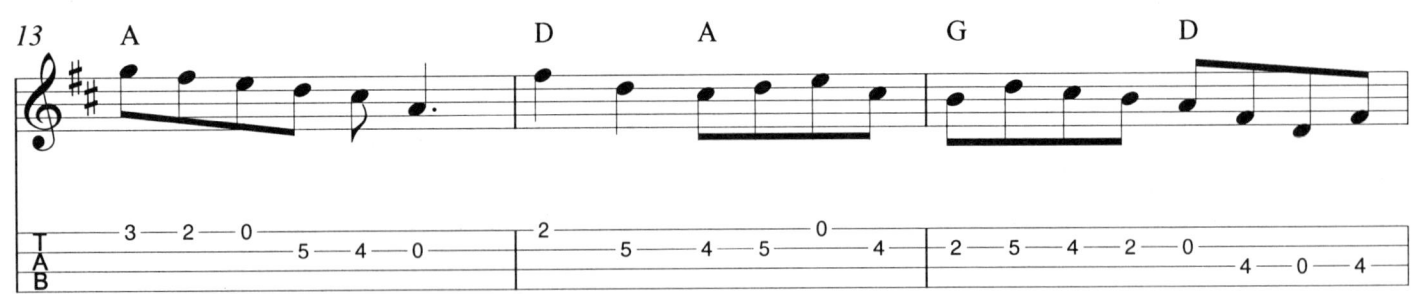